Voices in the Silence

Voices in the Silence

RUTH ANN FARMER

Xulon Press
2301 Lucien Way #415
Maitland, FL 32751
407.339.4217
www.xulonpress.com

Xulon
PRESS

© 2022 by Ruth Ann Farmer
Contributions by: Josina Hooks and Bre Goad
All rights reserved solely by the author. The author guarantees all contents are original and do not infringe upon the legal rights of any other person or work. No part of this book may be reproduced in any form without the permission of the author.

Due to the changing nature of the Internet, if there are any web addresses, links, or URLs included in this manuscript, these may have been altered and may no longer be accessible. The views and opinions shared in this book belong solely to the author and do not necessarily reflect those of the publisher. The publisher therefore disclaims responsibility for the views or opinions expressed within the work.

Unless otherwise indicated, Scripture quotations taken from The Message (MSG). Copyright © 1993, 1994, 1995, 1996, 2000, 2001, 2002. Used by permission of NavPress Publishing Group. Used by permission. All rights reserved.

Scripture quotations taken from the Good News Translation (GNT). Copyright © 1992 American Bible Society. Used by permission. All rights reserved.

Scripture quotations taken from the Holy Bible, New International Version (NIV). Copyright © 1973, 1978, 1984, 2011 by Biblica, Inc.™. Used by permission. All rights reserved.

Scripture taken from The Passion Translation (TPT). Copyright © 2017 by Passion & Fire Ministries, Inc. Used by permission. All rights reserved. thePassionTranslation.com

Paperback ISBN-13: 978-1-66286-363-9
Ebook ISBN-13: 978-1-66286-364-6

Table of Contents

Preface vii

Introduction ix

The Voice of Disappointment – Transforming Pain into a Positive Pathway 1

The Voice of Perspective – Transforming Tragedy into Triumph 9

The Voice of Rejection – Transforming Abandonment into Abiding Hope 15

The Voice of Bondage – Transforming Prisons by Self-Design into an Open Doorway of Purpose 21

The Voice of Condemnation – Transforming Failure into Faith 27

The Voice of Isolation – Transforming Emptiness into Fulfillment 35

The Voice of Insignificance – Transforming Despicable into Personal Value 39

The Voice of Chaos – Transforming Daily Details into Daily Deliverance 43

The Voice of Assumptions – Transforming Lies into Liberty 47

The Voice of Discouragement – Transforming Despair into Delight 51

Conclusion 55

Preface

Take a moment to pause and reflect on a situation in your life that literally made you feel "speechless." Perhaps it was observing an interaction at work of how a boss spoke to an employee, a parent-child interaction at a school sporting event, or even a verbal exchange between a husband and wife at church. You were shocked to see and hear the interaction, but felt awkward, fearful, or helpless to speak up in the middle of the situation, thinking it was "not your place" to get involved. Yet, your heart broke for the injustice you observed.

Voices in the Silence represents the internal thoughts, feelings, perspectives, and viewpoints from the experiences of a little girl as she entered the world and could only keep, in the silence of her heart, the internal conversations that she so earnestly desired to vocalize, but could not. When she entered her teen years, she began to journal her thoughts, worries, fears, and solutions to the challenges she faced and experienced. *Voices in the Silence* is her story of how pain was turned into discovering purpose and how God's promises were fulfilled in bringing a healing touch to her life, helping her realize that dreams do come true.

As an adult, I have had the joy of working with students who may have challenges with verbal or written expressive language due to a myriad of factors. I'm sure that growing up, I was extensively impacted by the impressions of my experiences and would have been identified as one with those challenges, as well.

How interesting now, as I see students grow and become extremely effective and precise in communicating with the appropriate supports and encouragement, that I, too, have learned to "share my story." It is my prayer that my journey will give you hope and courage to find your voice to speak, and to be freed from the chains and prison that the silence may strive to keep you trapped in. Truly, there is freedom and joy as you step out of the silence and share your journey.

These chapters will be a "snapshot" of a myriad of moments throughout my life and will not necessarily follow a consecutive order or timeline. As the Lord has recalled to the surface these buried memories, I will share to encourage and offer hope with the experiences He directs me to share. It's truly my prayer and hope that you will not only get a glimpse of His fingerprints and His handiwork in threading the details of my life for His glory, but to also open your eyes to see His plan and purpose for yours. Let the voices speak!

> *"Jesus said, 'No procrastination. No backward looks. You can't put God's kingdom off till tomorrow. Seize the day."* Luke 9:62

Today *is* the day to *stand up* and *speak up*. The Lord is my *voice*!

Introduction
Now That I Have Your Attention... It's Time to Speak Up

Really? You want me to do what? You know how busy I am! I'm not good at it, and... Yes, Lord, I know, I know, but... Okay, okay, no more excuses. I will stop putting You off, stop arguing, and receive the story You are writing. My life and my times are in Your hands. Here I am, Lord; please do this. I can't, but by Your power and for Your glory, Thy will be done.

Does this sound familiar? Do you, like me, ever "argue" with God? Well, here's the story He is writing:

"It's time, My child! People need the hope I offer. The voices need to be heard, for you are not alone, and I, your Father, have chosen your story to be a light of freedom to so many who walk the journey you have trod. The 'voices in the silence' must now be heard. I created you for a divine purpose. You matter, and your story will be a gateway of deliverance for others, just as I've set you free. I've got you and I will do this through you."

"I've given you My direction, as in Proverbs 31:8 (GNT): 'Speak up for people who cannot speak for themselves. Protect the rights of all who are helpless.' And in Proverbs 29:14 (MSG): 'Leadership gains authority and respect when the voiceless poor are treated fairly.'

*"Will you trust Me? You won't know the strength of your anchor until you've been in the storm. When on an excursion in a river raft on the rapids, you need a committed guide to see the stony rocks ahead to avoid the pitfalls and to triumphantly cross the finish line. I **am** your Anchor and your Guide."*

"Now is the time. Speak up and share the story I've created through you. Let the voices in the silence be heard!"

Yes, Lord! This is the reason You've placed me at the computer to write this story of encouragement, so others will know that *You* are the God of all hope, power, deliverance, and peace. I know You want to do for every person what You have done for me.

As I flashback on previous life episodes, I can see the faces and feel the emotions, but it's like watching a movie with muted sound, as the voices crying out from the scenes are silenced. The Lord has brought multiple buried memories to the surface, that I will share to encourage and offer hope in reflecting upon the journey He has brought me through.

Now That I Have Your Attention... It's Time to Speak Up

It is my passion that my journey will give you courage and strength to discover your own voice, and to speak and be freed from the chains and prison that the silence may strive to keep you trapped in. Truly, there is freedom and joy as you step out of the silence and share your journey. Oh, yes, and let Him write your story for *each life matters*! Your *best* days are ahead, awaiting you!

VOICES (in the) SILENCE Defined:

V – Victory
O – Overcomes
I – Inconveniences (that)
C – Challenge
E – Everyone's
S – Sanity

(in the)

S – Savior's
I – Intimate
L – Love
E – Encouraging
N – Never-ending
C – Compassion (and)
E – Enthusiasm

Reflection Questions:

1. Read Proverbs 31:8-9. *"Speak up for people who cannot speak for themselves. Protect the rights of all who are helpless. Speak up and judge fairly; defend the rights of the poor and needy."*

2. Journal the thoughts the Lord brings to your mind of someone He may place upon your heart to be the "voice in the silence" to speak up for them and to be the Lord's hands and feet to bring hope and encouragement to their life.

I
The Voice of Disappointment
Transforming Pain into a Positive Pathway

Day 1: December 27, 2017

As this first day of being sixty comes to a close, I must admit that it certainly has not followed the "plan" or the dreams that I had hoped *this day* would be like. However, it is with the greatest of joy that I am learning from my precious Lord and Savior that I have Him; therefore, I have *all* that I need.

> *"You, LORD, are all I have, and you give me all I need; my future is in your hands."* Psalm 16:5 (GNT)
> *"My grace is all you need. My power works best in weakness."* 2 Corinthians 12:9 (NLT)

"You may never know that Jesus is all you need, until Jesus is all you have." Corrie Ten Boom.

So, what did I hope today would be like? Well, please permit me to share my "dream day" for my sixtieth birthday that's been on my bucket list for some time. As I turn over a new decade, I had really hoped and dreamed that each new package of ten years would mark a memorable day, as well as the beginning of new changes and challenges for the following ten years to come. I wanted to experience several "firsts" to mark a memory of things I've never had the privilege and joy of ever doing previously.

For example, when I turned fifty, it was a huge delight and the most memorable experience to take my first cruise. I had *never* been on a large ship like the Disney Cruise Line, and I had not been out of the USA in over thirty years. The pure joy and sense of being delightfully overwhelmed by the grandeur of such an amazing cruise liner was truly awesome. To experience life out on the deep blue ocean and to visit Caribbean islands and the unique experiences they offer was phenomenal.

Let's come back to the present, and to this day of turning sixty years old. It had been my dream to take a trip to New York City, a place I've never been, and experience multiple facets of the big city life. I wanted to see the Broadway production of *Phantom of the Opera*, visit the Statue of Liberty, have lunch and shop at Tiffany's, and ice skate in Central Park, to name a few.

With reality in mind, here was how my day *actually* transpired. I woke up at least three times during the night, and even took pics to mark the timeline. I first woke up at 12:25 a.m.,

Transforming Pain into a Positive Pathway

but was able to fall back to sleep. I awoke again at 1:38 a.m., then 3:29 a.m. By 7:00 a.m., I got up again for the nightly bathroom run, and finally was up at 9:00 a.m. As I had my devotion and prayer time with the Lord, I fully surrendered this day (my birthday) to Him. I simply asked Him to guide me in His plan for the day and to make it memorable. I also asked that, if it be His will, I could experience at least one or two "firsts" to mark this special day.

As the day unfolded, I received one happy birthday wish from my son, who worked two hours away and couldn't get the day off, but had sent me a birthday present. A few hours later, a friend of twenty years texted me and wished me a happy birthday. Believing the Lord wanted me to maximize the gift of time for this day, I completed several tasks on my "to-do" list and felt good about bringing those to completion.

With the morning gone and only the afternoon left, I went out to return some Christmas items and decided to shop for a couple of needed items for my birthday. The Lord impressed upon my heart to invest this day in the lives of others, and that He would return the blessings in full. Thus, I actually bought a birthday gift for a little girl I knew when I saw a *My Little Pony* sleeping bag on a huge, discounted sale. It was energizing as I began to place my focus on what more I could do for others to invest my birthday for.

While I was driving, the Lord stopped me in my tracks when a song came on the radio titled "Your Love Defends Me" by Matt Maher. It so touched me that I had to text it to a precious family member who meant so much to me, as I wanted to encourage them in their life and ministry. Later, when I returned home, I couldn't stop playing the song. I played it over and over as the message on one hand broke my heart, but on the other hand, it was flooding my heart and spirit with amazing peace and joy. The Lord was re-assuring me of the promises in this song and from His Word.

The Lord was saying to me, *"Make this day and this song a 'first.' Make a video of yourself praising Me to remind yourself of the promises I'm giving you today on your sixtieth birthday."* So, this camera-shy gal did. In fact, the Lord so engulfed me in His arms through this song, that three times today at various moments of quietness, He would say, *"Do it again and again. I never want you to forget how I met you in a deeper way on this day. I am enough for you. You have Me; therefore, you have everything you need!"*

I had previously only made one planned visit for today, which was to take food to an older couple who I have known for twenty-five years, and who I loved and desired to take care of. Thus, when I stopped by, though the older gentleman was seventy-eight years old, he had gone out and bought some pizza and a cake for me. I was so touched! As I sat and listened to them telling stories of their past, simply observing the joy they had shared together over so many years, it was refreshing to experience life with them at this point in their journey. The Lord was saying again, *"Spend your birthday investing in the lives of others!"*

As I arrived home later that night, I again heard the Lord's voice say to me, *"Now, it's time for another 'first.' Go to your computer, the wonderful gift given to you from your son, and tell your story. You know, I've been putting this in your heart and mind for some time now, and* today *is the day to write the first pages."*

As it is 11:15 p.m. and my sixtieth birthday is coming to a close, I realize it was actually *just beginning*! Instead of this being a "day of firsts," the Lord had told me this would be a "year of firsts."

This is the motivation, heart, purpose, and passion for this writing: to let the world know and see that our loving Father in heaven has a plan and a purpose for each life. That every *pain* we may experience is the *pathway* to let our lives and our story be an encouragement to touch other lives, so that they, too, can know Him. That He loves them unconditionally and uses *every* detail (good and bad) in our lives to paint a masterpiece that draw others to Him.

Here's my story...

Permit the Lord to change your "PAIN" into a positive "PATHWAY."

P – Purposely
A – Arranging
I – Inconveniences (into)
N – New

P – Possibilities
A – And
T – Trusting
H – His
W – Wisdom (that)
A – Always (brings a)
Y – Yippee!

Reflection Questions:

1. Read Psalms 16:5 (GNT). *"You, LORD, are all I have, and you give me all I need; my future is in your hands."*

2. Journal the times you felt all alone and how the Lord met you in the situation, trial, or hardship. Let Him show you how He wants to bring healing and restore your joy, as He desires to turn your pain into a positive pathway that will bring hope to someone He wants your life to touch and encourage.

11
The Voice of Perspective
Transforming Tragedy into Triumph

The View: April 16, 2019

As I sit here looking upon the gorgeous Blue Ridge Mountains, the view is absolutely spectacular! I'm so humbly grateful and appreciative for the amazing friends the Lord has touched my life with to have the opportunity to enjoy such a beautiful place. Thank you, Jesus, for precious friends who have such beautiful, giving hearts and spirits.

The Lord brought to my mind the word "perspective" as I enjoy this view of His awesome creation. He has been asking me lots of questions to pause and reflect upon as I quietly reminisce upon His plan and the journey of my life. How did I view Him when I was a young child, when I experienced the challenging pathway of life's ups and downs, failures and victories? Then as a young adult when dreams were accomplished or dashed? Or now as a "more mature adult?" What am I trusting His view and plan to be for the next chapter of my life?

Let's take a moment to peel back the curtain of the past and look through the eyes of a three-year-old little girl. Though she couldn't verbalize the thoughts and fears she was feeling, she was emotionally expressing through her tears, *Daddy, Daddy... stop! I'm sorry... I won't cry any more. Please stop hurting me...,* as he came home again, drunk and abusing his little girl. *This* time, the scars would be permanent as he attacked her with a knife. He was so drunk that at least only her hand, not her face or body, was permanently scared. This is not to mention the emotional and relational scars pressed deeply into her soul, heart, mind, and spirit. Through this tragic experience of childhood abuse, did God have a plan, a purpose, and "perspective" for this little girl? Did He have a message of hope and deliverance to sow into her life?

Let's look at a year later, as she was now in the care of the state after having been placed in a children's home along with her younger sister. Her mother was unable to care for them as she had suffered polio and was left partially paralyzed; thus, she gave them up. Where was God when life seemed to go from bad to worse? Did she even know yet that God existed? That He was threading together the tragedies of her early years to create a message of hope in her to connect with future lives that God fully identified with the pain and heartache she experienced? That He would never waste a tragedy, but would completely "turn-it-around," to bring healing, hope, and the revelation of an intentional purpose and plan for every life, no matter what the journey may have been? He is a God who brings favor and blessing, anointing, increase, and abundance as we surrender every experience, every chapter of our lives, to His purpose and plan.

> *"He heals the broken in heart, and binds up their wounds."* Psalm 147:3 (NIV)
> *"Who redeems your life from the pit and crowns you with love and compassion."* Psalm 103:4 (NIV)
> *"Nevertheless, I will bring health and healing to it; I will heal my people and will let them enjoy abundant peace and security."* Jeremiah 33:6 (NIV)

So, what was next for this little girl? How was God going to bring healing and purpose into her life? Did He really care or was she just another statistic? Did her life really matter as some may view her life, devalue her worth, and deny her unique creation as God had intended?

Do we judge the wounded? Or are we His arms and feet to bring the hope of His love and goodness to those who are needing to experience the restoration and peace He desires to give? Pray for the Lord to rescue, redeem, renew, and restore His creation as each life matters!

Guess what happens next?

PERSPECTIVE Defined:

P – Providing
E – Every
R – Resource
S – So
P – Purpose
E – Extends
C – Continually
T – Toward
I – Intentional
V – Visionary
E – Experience

As I wrap up this chapter, the Lord plays a praise song I love on the radio: "The God of All My Days" by Casting Crowns. Wow, Lord! Thank you for Your timing and direction!

Reflection Questions:

1. Read 1 Corinthians 15:58. *"Therefore, my beloved brethren, be steadfast, immovable, always abounding in the work of the Lord, knowing that your toil is not in vain in the Lord."*

2. Read Titus 2:13-14. *"Looking for the blessed hope and the appearing of the glory of our great God and Savior, Christ Jesus, who gave Himself for us to redeem us from every lawless deed, and to purify for Himself a people for His own possession, zealous for good deeds."*

3. As you reflect upon your life's journey, take time to journal the Lord's timing in your life. What moments of tragedy did He use in His desire to transform them into opportunities of triumph? Perhaps you need to forgive and release past experiences, surrender them into His hands, and trust His plans for good to transform your perspective, and see how He promises to work *all* things together for your good and His glory (Romans 8:28).

III
The Voice of Rejection
Transforming Abandonment into Abiding Hope

A Silver Lining–The Thread of Connection: April 19, 2019

The weather! Whether you live in the Midwest, on a coastline with beautiful beaches, or in a remote mountain area, the weather typically provides the unexpected. As I take time to breathe in the spectacular Blue Ridge Mountains, the unexpected even makes its appearance here. From a gorgeous, stunning landscape view, the storms quickly roll in and the only view I have before me is heavy rain clouds, thunderstorms, and howling wind. Not to mention the sudden drop in temperature! When you live in Florida and you're accustomed to the nineties and one hundred percent humidity, then the temperature suddenly drops to forty-five degrees, the weather, the unexpected, has your full, undivided attention!

Isn't it interesting that many times the Lord needs to permit the unexpected to occur to get our attention and to cause us to stop and listen rather than running through our busy schedules, demands, commitments, and plans? Perhaps circumstances suddenly change, but no matter what, the Lord desires us to only look to Him for His intentional plans to be poured out in our daily lives, and to see how He is the connected thread who weaves His purposes into our lives all for His glory and our good.

Let's return to the story of our little four-year-old girl who found herself seemingly all alone in a children's home, and who quietly turned inward out of fear and abandonment. Did the Lord have a distinct plan and purpose in this setting? Was she forever to feel alone and forgotten? Was her life shattered with no hope for a place to call home or anyone to call family? Would she ever feel wanted, loved, or accepted? Was a new direction awaiting her as the Lord was weaving His perfect plan, in His perfect timing?

It never ceases to amaze me that when the Lord moves, He moves quickly. One specific day, a family showed up to visit the children's home. They had a little boy who was about eight-years-old, and they desired a daughter in their family as well as a sister for their little boy. When they walked in, our little girl was quietly playing on the floor with some toys. The little boy immediately sat down beside her and played with her. What fun it was for both of them! As the afternoon progressed, it became apparent to this little girl that this "new family" actually liked her and they wanted to take her home with them. Since her baby sister had already been previously adopted by another family, she was experiencing the feeling of being wanted for the first time. She was so happy to be placed in the car with her new family and drive to a new place she'd never seen or been to before.

Wow! How exciting as feelings began to flood her little heart and spirit. She even ate ice cream on the way to her new home. Her new parents couldn't understand why she couldn't hold a spoon and eat with it without making a mess, until she boldly took the spoon, placed it in her left hand, and devoured that delicious delicacy. Now they knew she was left-handed, and how that apparently insignificant detail would bring a specific purpose in the connected weave the Lord was designing. As she and her new big brother played in the back car window (wearing no seat belts was allowed then), she couldn't stop looking at him, the beautiful sky, and the new, approaching roadway. She began to talk a little again, as she had been given the gift of a family of her own.

The silver lining in the storms of the first four years of her life was becoming evident. The Lord had a plan to begin the healing process, though she didn't even know Him yet. How deeply He loves each and every one of us, and how He pursues us even when we don't even know of His existence. He is committed to His investment into His creation, love, and sacrifice so that we can come to know Him personally and intimately. He desires to bring healing to broken memories, to free us from the prisons of our past, and to place us upon a solid foundation of His Word, His promises, His power, and His provision!

Wow! Again, as His words flow through me, the song "Your Love Defends Me" by Matt Maher begins to play on the radio. Even at such a young age, a battle may have been raging, but He has won the battle and His defending love was always there, even though she felt all alone. He is the strength of our souls to protect and to defend. He is our salvation, our portion, and the provider of our every need.

As I look out the window now from this magnificent mountain cabin vantage viewpoint, the silver lining is peering through as the sun attempts to shine through the clouds and as the rain drifts off down the mountain side. What unexpected situations do you face? Are you willing to surrender the situation, the people, the heartbreak, the pain, the rejection, the anger, the failure, and whatever the "storm" may be, and trust that the loving Lord desires to use it to draw you closer to Him? Will you let Him bring healing, restoration, and clarity of the "silver lining" to connect you in a deeper walk with Him, and in revealing His divine purpose and plan in every unexpected experience?

SILVER LINING Defined:

S – Simply
I – Investing
L – Life
V – Values
E – Every day
R – Realizing (that the)

L – Lord
I – Is
N – Navigating
I – Instances (for)
N – Noteworthy
G – Growth

Reflection Questions:

1. Read 1 Peter 5:10 (NIV). *"And the God of all grace, who called you to his eternal glory in Christ, after you have suffered a little while, will himself restore you and make you strong, firm and steadfast."*

2. Read Romans 15:13. *"May the God of hope fill you with all joy and peace in believing, so that by the power of the Holy Spirit you may abound in hope."*

3. Spend some time in prayer and listen to how the Lord may want to encourage your heart to receive His healing and bring restoration to an area or relationship in your life. He does have a silver lining to bring a calm to the storm and to reveal His divine purpose for every situation. Journal His message of encouragement to you as a "point in time" of His faithfulness.

IV.
The Voice of Bondage
Transforming Prisons By Self-Design into an Open Doorway of Purpose

Prisons By Self-Design: April 19, 2019

As the song "Scars" by I AM THEY - Trial and Triumph is playing on the radio, I'm reminded of the scars that were inflicted on our little girl and how, in reflection as an adult, she needed to make some definite choices to either permit the past scars to dictate the pathway in life that she would choose or accept the freedom offered to her by the forgiveness and healing that the Lord provides. Would she lay down the old chains and embrace the new identity the Lord had designed for her?

How was our little girl now that she'd had a few years to adjust to her new home and family? Was it smooth sailing in her new setting? Were there challenges, disappointments, more pain, or a happy storybook ending? Let's peek in on her life's journey now at the age of eight-years-old.

Her new parents were committed church attenders and both had come to faith in Christ as their Savior. Growing up in church brought a combination of chains and freedoms for our little girl. Most importantly, when she was eight-years-old, a traveling evangelist was holding revival meetings at her church, and for the first time, she heard the gospel message. Sitting in her living room quietly at home, the Holy Spirit convicted her spirit. She realized she was a sinner, that Jesus died to pay for her sins, and she accepted Him as her Savior. It was a hallmark day! As she grew in her relationship with the Lord, He spoke truths to her spirit and heart as she fully surrendered her life to Him for His will, His way, and His service, for the plans He had for her life and future.

Though a church may teach, believe, and follow biblical principles, sometimes the daily practices may involve a legalistic approach, which hinders the relational building and interaction of fellowship with other believers. Unfortunately, you were a "good Christian" based upon dos and don'ts, more so than a practical expression of a moment-by-moment walk with Jesus. Chains of self-worth based upon dos and don'ts have a lasting effect and lead to an exterior performance of "Christ-likeness," rather than the interior attitude of who you are based upon the truth that God says we are.

Chains appear in a variety of forms, even for a believer in Jesus Christ: chains of doubt (losing your salvation, questioning the trustworthiness of the Lord), fear, insecurity, disappointment in unanswered prayers, accepting the perspectives of social media comments, believing the bullying comments/treatment from others as fact, or choosing to believe the lies of the enemy rather than the truth of the Word of the Lord. It's a daily walk and a daily perspective to continually seek the Lord, as to be aware of when we are walking "in chains" or walking "in freedom," and to let the scars of the past no longer dictate our daily beliefs and actions.

Living in a self-made prison and chains only leads to frustration, disappointment, anger, hatred, and a downward spiral in our life's journey. The daily monotony depletes our vitality, hope, and discernment of the voice of the Lord to our hearts. The enemy loves to keep us "trapped" in his world of lies. It's time to break free and let the name, power, and love of the Lord set you free. Truth equals freedom.

May you humble yourself at His feet, and embrace His forgiveness and freedom. He so desires you to embrace His love and plan for a fulfilling life. Each day is a new beginning to seek the Lord's discernment and wisdom that we are permitting the shadows of the past to fall away. The heartbreaks and scars should only serve as a reminder that He has carried us this far, and He has promised that *all things* will work together for our good. The past is a closed door, and His new open door awaits us each day. Are you ready to walk through the new open door? Why wait?

Prayer: (Brian Houston – Hillsong)

> "Lord, give me the courage to step outside of what is safe and comfortable as I trust You to cover me with Your all-sufficient grace. Holy Spirit, teach me how to grow my capacity to handle life's challenges, from a posture of trust and expectation of good. Thank You for Your faithfulness to me, even when I don't see it. You are my refuge and my strength, and with You, all things are possible!" (Matt. 19:26).

FREEDOM Defined:

F – Forever
R – Relying (on)
E – Eternal
E – Evidence (to)
D – Design (my)
O – Optimal
M – Motivation

Reflection Questions:

1. Read Matthew 19:26. *"Jesus looked at them and said, 'With man this is impossible, but with God, all things are possible.'"*

2. Reflect upon the Lord's promise and jot down in your journal the areas in your life where you need the Lord's deliverance to "break the chains," and put yourself on a pathway of freedom as you begin a new chapter and journey.

V.
The Voice of Condemnation
Transforming Failure into Faith

Mother's Day: May 13, 2018

I'll be honest... It took me several hours to get here, following multiple conversations with my Father and maximizing a myriad of excuses of "things to be done" since my "to-do" list is *so* long, as the end of the school year is rapidly approaching. He won! I'm finally sitting where He's been ever so gently nudging me to go, which is back to the computer, and His opportunity to write another chapter in the story He's writing in the book of my life. It is also an opportunity for me to surrender to His plan with obedience and joy as I am right back where He so desires me to be *much more often...* sitting at His feet and listening to His voice.

Today is Mother's Day, which historically is a day to honor and shower our mothers with love, gratitude, and praise for who they are and for all that they have done to impact our lives. It is a day that certainly every mother deserves, but not necessarily embraces. You see, though we rejoice with each mom, and for the blessings each one experiences in the journey of motherhood as their children grow to become mature, productive, contributing members of society — ideally, those who have discovered their value, potential, giftedness, and calling that the Lord has put on each life — this is not the experience of a multitude of moms. This even goes for those who strive to raise their children in biblical principles, and purposes the Lord has for each life.

Thus, my journey to this day of motherhood brings a flood of emotions. Please permit me to share a glimpse into my pathway of being a mom. I must begin by retrieving a memory of when our little girl was around ten years old. She was highly influenced by her pastor's wife, who was such a role model in her life of what a Godly wife and a mother should be like. Our little girl would never forget her and the impact she made upon her life. She remembered only having one motivating drive in her life as to the calling the Lord placed upon her to be a wife and a mother, and to raise Godly children who walked with Him. This truly was her passion and goal as she was growing up.

At a very young age, the Lord already had her babysitting for multiple families. She was teaching Sunday School and Vacation Bible School at the age of twelve, as the Lord grew her love to be that of working with children. She worked in summer camps, led a community area youth group called "Conquerors for Christ," to recall some of the investments in how the Lord was preparing her for the journey ahead, and to invest her life in growing children. She was *so* excited in anticipating the day when He would let her become a mom.

Now, please permit me to fast-forward to today, Mother's Day. For many moms, this is a day of heartbreak as they pray daily for their children that the Lord will rescue, redeem, renew, and restore them to a relationship with Him. Though they did their very best to diligently follow the Lord's leading in raising them, and in being an example and role model, they still so desperately desire for them to know an intimate relationship with the Lord. Yet, each one still must make their own choices, and by so doing, the life each child chooses to embrace.

Mothers, it can be difficult to reflect on your children on this day. For example, as moms have shared their stories with me, their child may live on the opposite side of the country, rarely contacting them and escaping the pain of life in their journey by hiding in a gold mine or wallowing in anger, bitterness, and resentment. Or perhaps you have a child who has lived on the streets all across the country, and who randomly shows up unexpectedly, which, of all weeks, happened to me this week.

I stayed late at school in an attempt to whittle down the stack of paperwork on my desk. As I was leaving the building and heading to my car, I heard a voice call out and looked across the street. I saw a couple of workers attempting to get a leaf blower working, and assumed it was them. Their blower kept stopping and in that moment of quietness, I heard a voice calling out again. I turned around to look in the direction of the voice, and still only saw the two men working on the leaf blower. Thus, I ignored the voice, got into my car, and headed down the street.

As I headed toward the stop sign, I was paralyzed with fear when I saw a tall, lanky figure walking toward me who looked ever-so-familiar. I immediately looked in the opposite direction, pulled down the sun visor, and sped away. As I looked back in the rearview mirror, I knew it was my long-lost child, and it was his voice that was calling out "Mom." Due to his prior at-risk behaviors, I was counseled to not have contact with him for my own protection and safety. Although that small voice always tugged at my heart, making me think that perhaps "this time" would be different. Perhaps "this time" he would be restored. Being alone in that moment and being overcome with fear, I drove on, condemning myself for fear and lack of faith.

Thus, as a mom on Mother's Day, I fully understand the diverse feelings and emotions that women all across the country may be experiencing today. Though, in the depths of our "mother's heart," we all have wished for and have prayed that our children would pursue Him. We can only do our best before we must leave them in His hands. So, dear, precious moms, I must encourage you and remind you that you *are loved,* you *are valued*, and you have *not failed*. Rather, you must remember that your children are not yours, but were only entrusted to you for a time, and that His plans and purposes will prevail.

Please don't beat yourselves up. Rather, find grace and peace in the Lord, knowing that you've done all you can, that the Lord is still on the throne, and His purposes for your good and His glory are to *win*! You are a winner, a rock star, and He is pleased with you. He loves you unconditionally because that's His character. He is good, faithful, full of compassion, and He walks with you. He carries you in His arms daily. His strength and promises meet your every need no matter what!

Continue to fill your heart, mind, and soul with the promises in Scripture, and with songs of worship and praise. He is your victor, and He will bring victory into the lives of your children.

FAITH Defined:

F – Forever
A – Available
I – In
T – Trustworthiness (and)
H – Hope

Reflection Questions:

1. Read Ephesians 3:20 (NIV). *"Now to him who is able to do immeasurably more than all we ask or imagine, according to his power that is at work within us."*

2. Humbly pray and leave in His hands all failures. Stand up and speak up for, in the voice of faith, the promises He will accomplish as you trust in Him. Record in your journal this date and step of faith, believing Him to do abundantly beyond all that you think. He is able!

STAND UP (and) SPEAK UP Defined:

S – Steadfast
T – Trust (with)
A – Abiding
N – Non-negotiable
D – Dependence

U – Upon (God's)
P – Promises

(and)

S – Sincerely
P – Proclaim
E – Eternal
A – And
K – Kind

U – Uplifting
P – Powerful (words)

> Read Isaiah 41:10. *"Fear not, for I am with you; be not dismayed, for I am your God; I will strengthen you; I will help you; I will uphold you with my righteous right hand."*

VI.
The Voice of Isolation
Transforming Emptiness into Fulfillment

The Lord Closes the "Doggie" Chapter: July 26, 2018

I moved closer to the "moving day" out of the house, since the Lord had sold the house in four days. Though I still had no place to move into yet, the Lord had made this day as the anointed day to close the chapter on my "doggie connection."

Today, I gave away Ziggy, who had been with me for approximately ten years. I got him in the spring, May, I think, following the February passing of my mother. I got Miss D the following year. I got Aiko a few weeks following her birth. She weighed one and a half pounds when I got her. I have been her only owner until today. She was with me for seven years.

With the sale of this house and the need to find a place to rent — which was extremely difficult if you had pets — especially *three* doggies (though all together, they weighed a total of approximately fifteen pounds,) which was much less than some people's pets, who only have one dog.

Moving was also hard on the dogs, to keep making the adjustments to another new location. Thus, the Lord began to gently work on my heart (for He knows how much I love my doggies) to be willing to give them away. I began to pray for a family who would not only take all three of them and keep all three together, but who truly would love and care for them as much as I did. In the Lord's amazing faithfulness, He provided that family within the past week. A lady I worked with at school heard about my need to find them a good home, and her family came to visit (interview my doggies) to see if they were a good fit for their family, since they had two children, ages eight and three. Also, my co-worker's sister lived with the family and she was interested in having a doggie, too.

When they came to visit, it was amazing to watch my doggies interact and engage with the family and the children. Not once did my doggies bark or act fearful or hesitant. Rather, they seemed to connect in a way that had never happened before when my doggies met new people. Usually, they barked profusely, attempted to snip at their ankles, or ran to me for safety. *Not* so with this family.

So, they were the Lord's provision! This family only lived seven minutes from my house, and as I drove, I was struggling with saying goodbye. The Lord had His song for me playing on the radio that *He* gave me back in February when I walked back into this house and found it in total disarray. The song, called "The God of All My Days," began to play, and I knew He was ordering my steps "this day" to pass the baton (doggies) on to another precious family, knowing they'd be well-cared for, and permitting the Lord to "close this chapter" in my life's journey.

Later, when I arrived back home and was truly all alone, the Lord, again, faithfully had the radio play "Your Love Defends Me," which reminded me of my birthday, the time when He gave me that song as a comfort to know that I never really was alone, as He truly was always with me. Though I cried in the emptiness of the doggies' love for me now being gone, the Lord always filled the empty spots with Himself, and *He was enough*!

He also reminded me that with the closure of this doggie chapter of my life, He'd bring even *greater* days ahead to not only fill the empty places, but to fill my life to over-flowing with His great delights that He had in His plans to bless me.

Thank you, Lord Jesus! My Heavenly Father loves continually!

FULFILLMENT Defined:

F – Faithfully
U – Uploading
L – Loving
F – Favor (and)
I – Instilling
L – Life
L – Long
M – Motivation (for)
E – Eternal
N – Non-Perishable
T – Treasures

Reflection Questions:

1. Read Psalms 91. Reflect on where your thoughts and feelings go when you find yourself all alone. Yes, people may be all around you, but is anyone aware of your loneliness and isolation within?

2. Are you angry, resentful, or bitter at the situation(s) you find yourself facing?

3. Are you willing to surrender and embrace the intimacy of the presence of our loving Heavenly Father, and rest in His plans to fill your heart, spirit, and soul?

VII.
The Voice of Insignificance
Transforming Despicable into Personal Value

Miss D's Story: August 4, 2018

In Matthew 10:29b, God's Word says that He cares for the least of these, and even knows when a sparrow falls. Though Miss D was most definitely *not* a sparrow, to me she was *so* loved and valued as one of my precious doggies. Today, the Lord so amazingly demonstrated how much He cared, even for the "least of these."

Only ten days ago, the Lord provided a family who took all three of my precious "doggies," but due to Miss D's special needs, they felt they couldn't care for her. Miss D had issues with bladder control and she had a weak hip, which made her limp when she walked. Though I couldn't take her back due to the timeline with moving again and that fact I was *not* allowed to have pets established by my contract where I was moving, the family begged for me to come get her. I assured them that I was actively looking for another new home for her, but hadn't found one yet. I reminded them that she could not come back to this house I was temporarily in, as it had been sold, and I had to move out.

Well, today, I got a text that I must come to get Miss D by tomorrow. As I continued to pray, the Lord brought to my mind my mover, who had taken Bo, my bird, when we moved out of the townhouse. The mover had also added a new friend named Daisy to his cage/home, and now the Lord directed me to reach out to this family and see if they would want Miss D.

The Lord continued to amaze me by *His faithfulness* to care, and to provide for even the "little things" that I cared about. *Again*, when God moves, He moves quickly! Within five minutes of getting the text, the Lord provided a new home for her! *Thank you, precious Heavenly Father!*

Not only did He provide for Miss D, but He *again* had yet another of His songs for me playing on the radio, which had consistently been there when I needed to hear it. The radio was playing "Masterpiece" by Danny Gokey at the right moment. Wow! How intimately the Lord knows our hearts and concerns, and how He *so much* desires to let us know *how much He really cares and loves us!* I was humbled and so touched by His love for me, and for caring about what matters to me.

I love You, Lord!

Transforming Despicable into Personal Value

VALUED Defined:

V – Viewing
A – Affectionately (with)
L – Lifelong (and)
U – Unmeasurable
E – Eternal
D – Devotion

Reflection Questions:

1. Do you ever feel you have areas in your life that make you feel despicable, unworthy, and unloved? Just as Miss D was experiencing weaknesses and less than desirable qualities, she was loved and valued to her very last day on this earth. I received a phone call on January 14, 2020 that she passed away. To hear the tears and compassion in the voice of her owner who only had a brief year to love her for who she was, with all of her faults, truly touched my heart.

2. Just think: if we as humans can care so deeply for a doggie, imagine how deep and outreaching our Heavenly Father's love is for you, no matter what! *You* are so valuable to Him.

VIII.
The Voice of Chaos
Transforming Daily Details into Daily Deliverance

Freedom Day: August 15, 2018

Today, the Lord broke the chains of another "past chapter" by finalizing the closing of the house. As I entered the house for the last time, He reminded me of the spot in the living room where He met me back on May 2, 2018. That day was when I first entered this house and found it a total disaster, but He assured me that He was ordering my steps and my days. As I stood in that same spot for the last time, I thanked Him for how He so miraculously used pain from the past, and now turned it to break the chains, setting me free from a huge financial burden that had been placed on me.

The past four days have been intense, to say the least, putting in eighteen-plus hour days to get moved out of the house, finish painting projects, and clean thoroughly for the buyers to do their final walk-through in preparation for the closing today. Multiple last-minute challenges occurred, but the Lord kept saying, "I *am* the *victor*, and I have *won*."

"God's glory is all around me! His wrap-around presence is all I need, for the Lord is my Savior, my hero, and my life-giving strength." Psalms 62:7 (TPT)

As I drove away and said goodbye to the strong and solid, twenty-foot tree that I had planted there as a tiny six-foot branch approximately fifteen years ago, the Lord gave me encouragement that if He had taken care of "my tree," *He* will certainly take care of me. When driving home, the Lord so faithfully, and at the perfect time, had my song He'd given me for this journey play on the radio, "The God of All My Days." All I could do was cry and praise Him again for His love, goodness, faithfulness, and intimate care for me.

DELIVERANCE Defined:

D – Daily
E – Equipping
L – Lives
I – In
V – Victory
E – Even
R – Rearranging
A – And
N – Navigating
C – Circumstances
E – Effectively

Reflection Questions:

1. Ponder a difficulty or an impossible challenge you have faced. How did God's deliverance show up? How will you surrender and trust by faith that He is working all details together for your good and His glory in His perfect timing?

2. If you feel like God has let you down and hasn't brought deliverance yet, what lesson(s) is He wanting you to understand while you continue to "wait and believe" in His promise to deliver you?

IX.
The Voice of Assumptions
Transforming Lies into Liberty

Perception/Perspective: December 1, 2019

Interesting, isn't it? When the Lord places a desire on your heart, a directive that opens the doors to the next chapter in your life, and yet, it was nearly 10:00 p.m., and the *last* thing I finally sat down to do — after having a week off — feels like I have *too* many items on my "to-do" list. Priorities. My wish when my week off began was to spend time writing more chapters in this book and yet, how difficult it seemed to be to make myself actually go to the computer, sit down and let His words flow. So many excuses in why I didn't get here sooner, or why I permitted other demands to occupy my time. It seemed so difficult to get here and yet, now that I was here, my heart and spirit instantly began to *soar* with *joy* as I was doing the very thing that He'd desired me to do. Lord, please give me Your drive and strength to always go first where You are calling me to be and do what You are wanting me to do.

Voices in the Silence

As I'd been reflecting on "perspective," the Lord had given me so many thoughts and viewpoints to ponder. He frequently reminded me that it was so important to know the backstory before drawing assumptions or conclusions about the whole story. In this day and age of instant everything, I seemed to have frequent interactions with individuals who either assumed a conclusion about an individual based on extremely limited information, and thus, they "never judged," but frequently assumed a perspective about someone without even beginning to know or understand the what, where, when, and why about a given person or situation. People may have claimed to "never judge," but they certainly drew assumptions/conclusions based on incomplete or limited information, if it's even actually, factually true. It's *so* important to not confuse the "facts" with the "truth." People may give you a response, but not an answer.

In Proverbs 15:23 (MSG), it says, *"A person finds joy in giving an apt reply — and how good is a timely word!"* This chapter continues to emphasize that *"the heart of the righteous weighs its answers."* Thus, to be the victorious warrior, our role is to encourage, support, and serve others, even those who may have a completely inaccurate perspective about who we are, our heart's motivations, and passions that drive our words and actions.

> *"Smart people know how to hold their tongue;*
> *their grandeur is to forgive and forget."*
> Proverbs 19:11 (MSG)

> *"Don't jump to conclusions — there may be a perfectly good explanation for what you just saw."* Proverbs 25:8 (MSG)

Heavenly Father, forgive them, for they know not the impact (fallout) of what they do should be our prayer. We can only control our responses to others, and we need to be intentional in our interactions to be continually surrendered to the Holy Spirit so that others only see in and through us, our words and our actions, a reflection of the hands and feet, the words, and responses of Jesus. This is our mission and our pathway to freedom. Our communication, our delivery, our character, and our lives should always reflect His life and truth.

LIBERTY Defined:

L – Living
I – Intentionally (with)
B – Biblical
E – Energy (to)
R – Respond (with)
T – Tender
Y – Yearnings

Reflection Questions:

1. How do you respond when others say or do things that could be an offense, a put down, or an attack on your character, simply because they appear to "assume" they know a detail about you that is not even close to the truth, or at least is an inaccurate representation of who you are or a misinterpretation of something you may have said or done? Write down the experience on paper, pray, and ask the Lord to give you His power to forgive, and to realize that we tend to view/see others or situations through an unclear lens.

2. Ask the Lord for His wisdom and discernment in every situation so that you see through the eyes of others' perspectives, and be sure to get "all the information" before arriving at a conclusion. Write down words you can say or actions that you can do to follow biblical instructions of using our words at a timely opportunity, to be an encouragement to others.

X.
The Voice of Discouragement
Transforming Despair into Delight

"Pie" Day: March 14, 2019

Dream, Girl (Dream as a verb, *not* an adjective)

Well, it's "Pi" day. Yes, in the world of education, it's all about the "math formulas," but for me, today is "Pie" Day. It was so much more invigorating to actually permit myself the pleasure of eating an *actual* piece of pie! Yummy, for sure!

Though most at school had "pie" on the brain today, the Lord had an amazingly different plan and purpose for *this* particular day. At the end of the school day, following multiple hours over many days, I finally was able to drop off my tax papers/info with my tax lady, Amanda. You see, when I first met Amanda six years ago, the Lord was initiating a long-term connection so that His light could bring encouragement to the darkness and challenges in her life.

Today, as I was driving to her work, about an hour's drive, the Lord was flooding my heart with joy over the miraculous life-saving experience of a friend whose son spent about four days in the ICU, made a turn for the upswing, and the parents texted us to let us know of his twenty-four-hour turn around at the exact moment our entire school body was praying for him in chapel. The Lord began the healing process, and the son would now live instead of moving into eternity.

As I arrived at Amanda's work, I gave her a big hug, and her first response was, "Wow, you smell *so* good!" I blushingly thanked her, and we began our usual, annual catch-up conversations. About an hour later, as I was getting ready to leave, I hugged her again and she noted the lovely smell. I immediately opened my purse and pulled out a tiny bottle of perfume. It was an "after Christmas" sale purchase, and it had come with three small bottles in the package. As I pulled it out of my purse, I immediately handed it to her. She was pleasantly surprised and loved that it was actually a roll-on, not a spray. When she read the name of the perfume on the bottle, it became another opportunity to share the Lord's encouragement for her personal family challenges, and she was *so* thrilled that it was called "Dream Girl."

Most read that title and instantly thought, *Oh, you are a dream girl. The perfect vision of what a gorgeous girl looks like, how she appears and looks "so perfect."* The joy in this moment of giving my friend the perfume was her response of "Dream Girl." Be sure to live in hope and with the anticipation of answered prayers that the Lord is and will be at work to solve every challenge you're facing. She was so encouraged to keep believing and to keep dreaming for the good plans and solutions the Lord would provide.

It was truly another moment of experiencing the joy of the Lord, in being His servant and bringing hope and encouragement to a hurting world. How exhilarating it was to sing and worship Him all the way driving home.

> *"Now, may God, the fountain of hope, fill you to overflowing with uncontainable joy and perfect peace as you trust in him. And may the power of the Holy Spirit continually surround your life with his super-abundance until you radiate with hope!"* Romans 15:15 (TPT)

No matter what we may be experiencing, we can always be the Lord's hands and feet to bring joy to others. In fact, our joy grows as we focus on Him, surrender our concerns to Him, and watch and wait with expectancy to see all that *He will do*! *Dream on!*

DELIGHT Defined:

D – Delivering
E – Expressions (of)
L – Love
I – In
G – Giving
H – Hope
T – To (others)

Reflection Questions:

1. Read Romans 15:1-13, then ask yourself the following questions. Do I take the time to notice the little things? Am I aware of the opportunities to encourage others to dream and believe? Am I a hope builder?

2. Write down the names of three people you can encourage today. Perhaps a text, a phone call, or even a written note of gratitude is just the delight you can bring to someone else today.

Conclusion
More Voices

Let's take a few moments to reflect and sneak a peek into a myriad of moments that our little girl experienced, where the Lord was designing and equipping her to speak up. Though, at the moments of these episodes, she could only remain silent. How would the Lord transform messes into miracles? How would He take every situation and use it for His glory and her good? In Romans 8:28 (TPT), He promises, *"So we are convinced that every detail of our lives is continually woven together for good, for we are his lovers who have been called to fulfill his designed purpose."*

What was her life like as she began to dream of a new life? As she spent hours in her rope swing that hung from the large cottonwood tree near the chicken house?

Did she have challenges in school as she walked the mile and a half down the country dirt road to attend a "one-room schoolhouse" with two kids in her grade? Wow! Yes, she was privileged to spend her early educational years in one of the last remaining country schoolhouses, with kiddos in kindergarten all the way through eighth grade. Oh, yes, the lessons experienced indeed!

Did she have friends or was she still all alone in her world of fears and doubts, as she spent each evening in the barn milking the cows, feeding the chickens, and pigs?

How was the Lord touching her heart and teaching her spirit to see and understand from His perspective? How was He truly building and equipping her to not only grow in her love and understanding of Him, but to begin to remove the "blinders" and see the exciting pathway that awaited her?

Keep seeking Him, His Word, and His plan and purpose *each* day! Exciting days await as she shares more of *His story* that He's writing with her life, and as she has *great joy* in learning to *speak up* and *stand up* with others to share the Lord's amazing handiwork and purpose for their lives! *More to come*!

CPSIA information can be obtained
at www.ICGtesting.com
Printed in the USA
BVHW020425170123
656278BV00024B/2526